MY FIRST BOOK

BERMUDA

ALL ABOUT BERMUDA FOR KIDS

GLOBED
CHILDREN BOOKS

Interior and cover Design: Daniel Day
Editor: Margaret Bam

For My Sons, Daniel, David and Jude

Bermuda Bay, Bermuda

Bermuda

Bermuda is an island territory.

An island territory is a **region that is surrounded by water and is governed as a separate entity from other nearby regions.**

Territories have their own unique cultures, languages, and political systems, while still maintaining some level of affiliation with their governing countries or territories.

St. George's, Bermuda

Where Is Bermuda?

Bermuda is geographically located in the continent of **America**.

A continent is **a massive area of land that is separated from others by water or other natural features**.

Bermuda is situated in **North Atlantic Ocean.**

Hamilton, Bermuda

Capital

The capital of Bermuda is **Hamilton.**

Hamilton is located on the **main island of the territory, which is also called Bermuda.**

Hamilton is also the largest city in Bermuda.

Tobacco Beach, Bermuda

Parishes

Bermuda is divided into nine parishes

The parishes of Bermuda are

1. Devonshire
2. Hamilton
3. Paget
4. Pembroke
5. St. George's
6. Sandys
7. Smith's
8. Southampton
9. Warwick

Population

Bermuda has population of around **64,000 people.**

Bermuda is the second-most populous of the British overseas territories, after the Cayman Islands.

Crystal Cave, Bermuda

Size

Bermuda is **53.20 km2.** Despite its small size, Bermuda is known for its beautiful pink-sand beaches, coral reefs, and distinctive blend of British and African cultural influences.

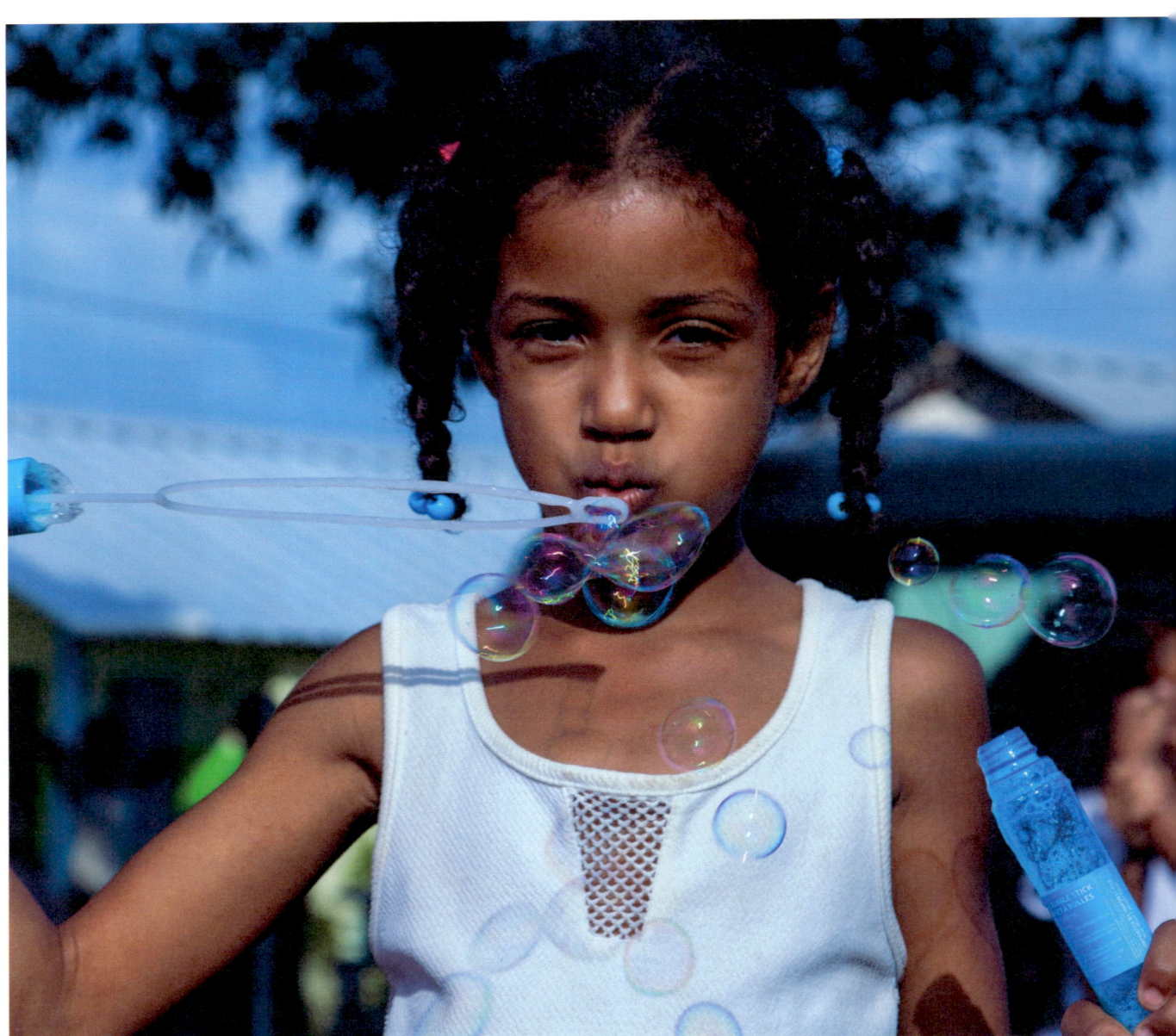

Languages

The official language of Bermuda is English. Standard English is used in professional settings and in writing, while vernacular Bermudian English is spoken on more casual occasions.

Here are a few phrases in Bermudian English
- **Wopnin - Short for "what's happening"**
- **Jet - Going somewhere quickly.**
- **Ace Boy or Ace Girl - Best Friend**
- **Chingas - You say this when you're surprised or you want to say 'wow'.**

Gibbs Hill Lighthouse

Attractions

There are lots of interesting places to see in Bermuda.

Some beautiful places to visit in Bermuda are

- **Crystal and Fantasy Caves**
- **Gibb's Hill Lighthouse**
- **Bermuda Aquarium, Museum and Zoo**
- **Royal Naval Dockyard**
- **Horseshoe Bay**

Somerset Village, Bermuda

History of Bermuda

Bermuda has a fascinating history. Bermuda was first discovered by Spanish navigator Juan de Bermúdez in 1505, but it was not until 1609 that the English established a permanent settlement on the island.

In the 19th century, Bermuda became a popular destination for tourists.

Bermuda remained a British colony until 1968, when it became a self-governing British Overseas Territory.

Woman in Bermuda

Customs in Bermuda

Bermuda has many fascinating customs and traditions.

- Bermudians are known for their friendly and welcoming hospitality. They also have a strong sense of community and are proud of their island's unique culture and traditions.
- Bermuda is home to a number of colourful festivals and traditions, including the annual Cup Match cricket tournament, the Christmas Boat Parade, and the Easter Kite Festival.

Collie Buddz

Music of Bermuda

Bermuda has a vibrant music scene that includes a variety of genres. Some of the popular music genres in Bermuda include **jazz, reggae, soca, calypso, and hip-hop.**

Some notable Bermudian musicians include
- **Collie Buddz - A Bermudian reggae artist best known for his single "Come Around".**
- **Heather Nova - A Bermudian singer-songwriter and poet.**

Bermudian fish chowder

Food of Bermuda

Bermuda is famous for its vibrant, delicious and rich food.

The national dish of Bermuda is **fish chowder**, a hearty soup made with fish, tomatoes, onions, garlic, and herbs.

Food of Bermuda

Bermudian cuisine is a blend of British, African, and Caribbean influences.

Some popular dishes in Bermuda include

- **Bermuda fish sandwich: A sandwich made with fried fish fillets.**
- **Peas n' rice: A staple side dish made with rice and peas cooked in coconut milk and flavored with spices and herbs.**
- **Rum cake: A moist, dense cake made with Bermuda rum, eggs, butter, and spices, and typically served with a dollop of whipped cream.**

The Bermuda Cenotaph, Hamilton, Bermuda

Weather in Bermuda

Bermuda has a subtropical climate with mild temperatures throughout the year.

The average high temperature ranges from 70°F in the winter to 85°F in the summer.

Sea Turtles

Animals of Bermuda

Bermuda is home to a diverse range of wildlife.

Here are some of the beautiful animals found in Bermuda

- Humpback Whales
- Bermuda Petrel
- Bermuda Buckeye Butterfly
- Bermuda Cave Shrimps
- Land Hermit Crabs
- Bermuda Longtails
- Sea Turtles

Horseshoe Bay Beach, Bermuda

Beaches

There are many beautiful beaches in Bermuda which is one of the reasons why so many people visit this beautiful country every year.

Here are some of Bermuda's beaches

- **Clearwater Beach**
- **John Smith's Bay Beach**
- **Horseshoe Bay Beach**
- **Tobacco Bay**
- **Jobson's Cove Beach**

Sports of Bermuda

Sports play an integral part in Bermudian culture. The most popular sports in Bermuda are **association football, athletics and cricket.**

Here are some of famous sportspeople from Bermuda

- **Flora Duffy - Athletics**
- **Clarence Hill - Boxing**
- **Reggie Lambe - Football**
- **Khano Smith - Football**

Bermuda Flag

Famous

Many successful people hail from Bermuda.

Here are some notable Bermudian figures

- **Dwayne Leverock - Cricketer**
- **Mishka - Musician**
- **George Tucker – Attorney**
- **Ewart Brown – Politician**
- **Lena Headey – Actress**

Hamilton, Bermuda

Something Extra...

As a little something extra, we are going to share some lesser known facts about Bermuda

- **Bermuda is home to a rare bird called the Bermuda Petrel, also known as the Cahow. The bird was once thought to be extinct, but a small population was discovered in 1951.**
- **Bermuda has a thriving art scene, with a number of galleries and studios showcasing the work of local and international artists.**

Dockyard, Bermuda